A Gift for Grandpa

Written and illustrated by Rebecca Ashdown

CW01401274

RISING STARS

Jim kicks the ball.
Grandpa kicks the ball back.

Yes! I can still run and shoot!

Clap!
Clap!

Grandpa is just as quick as Jim.

Grandpa will be 70 soon.

Jim has a plan.

His mum and dad help.

Gran is in on the plan too!

Today Grandpa is 70.

Jim has a gift for Grandpa.

Hello!

Clap!

Clap!

A ball is the best gift for Grandpa!

Talk about the story

Ask your child these questions:

1 Who was playing football at the start of the story?

2 Who was going to be 70 soon?

3 Who knew about Jim's plan?

4 Why was a ball the best gift for Grandpa?

5 How old are the people you live with?

6 What is the best gift you've ever given someone?

Can your child retell the story in their own words?